E
DIOP, Birago
Mother Crocodile

Mother Crocodile

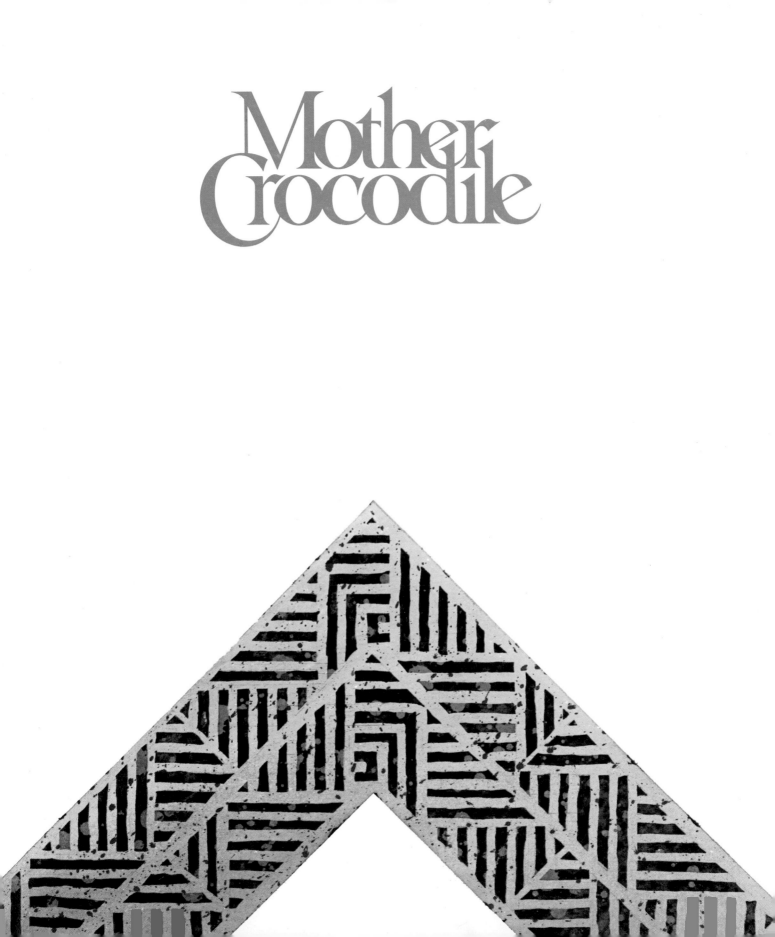

Mother Crocodile

"MAMAN-CAÏMAN" BY BIRAGO DIOP

Translated and adapted by Rosa Guy
Illustrated by John Steptoe

DELACORTE PRESS/NEW YORK

Published by
Delacorte Press
1 Dag Hammarskjold Plaza
New York, N.Y. 10017

"Maman-Caïman," an Ouolof folk tale from Senegal, West Africa,
appeared in *Les Contes d'Amadou Koumba* by Birago Diop.

Manufactured in the United States of America.

First printing

Library of Congress Cataloging in Publication Data

Diop, Birago.
Mother Crocodile=Maman-Caïman

SUMMARY: Because Mother Crocodile tells stories of the past, the little crocodiles
choose to believe she is crazy until they learn otherwise.
[I. Guy, Rosa. II. Steptoe, John. III. Title.]
PZ8.1D59Mo   398.2′452798′09663   [E]   80-393

ISBN 0-440-06405-8
ISBN 0-440-06406-6 (lib. bdg.)

To—Didier, Chief, Quasy, Quamy, Avatar, Jojo,
Abdou, Doudou, to all my other little friends,
and to Alioune Diop.

"'Of all the animals that fly in the air, walk on the earth, or swim in the water, the craziest must be the crocodiles, who creep on the earth and walk on the bottoms of rivers.'

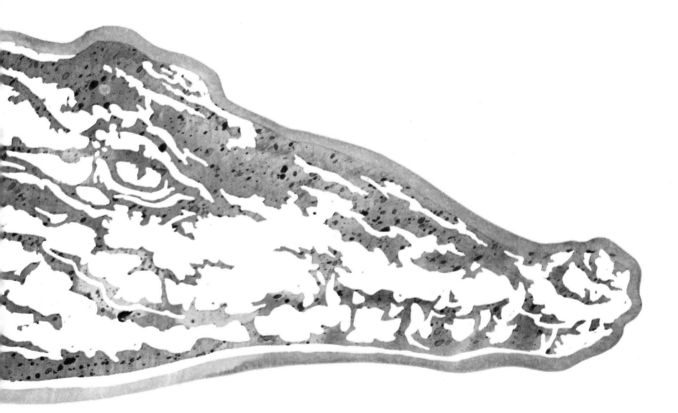

"Of course that is not my opinion," said Uncle Amadou, the storyteller. He sat on a rock in front of his grass house talking to the village children. "It is the opinion of Golo. That monkey has a vicious tongue." Uncle Amadou lit his pipe.

"We know how wicked Golo can be. He goes around spreading gossip about everyone! But you must remember that when brains were given out, Golo stood at the end of the line. He received the smallest portion."

Uncle Amadou puffed his pipe slowly. The children waited patiently. He was a very wise man.

"Golo said that crocodiles were the craziest of all animals. Then he said Dia, Mother Crocodile, had the best memory in the world. It seemed as if Golo were praising Mother Crocodile, but what he really meant was that Dia lived in the past. And what he really wanted was revenge. She had snapped at him once because he had been teasing her.

"So it is safe to say that Golo said what he did to get even with Dia.

"It was true that Dia had a good memory. She might even have had the best memory on earth.

"All day long she would look up from the slimy waters of the river where she swam or from the shining sands of its banks where she took the sun. She heard many tales of animals and men.

"She learned the news that the riverboat paddles told to the fish. And the fish gossiped, too, as they traveled down the great rivers to the sea, where the sun swims to end its day.

"Dia also listened to the chatter of the women who washed their clothes in the river.

"She listened to the donkeys and camels, too. When they traveled from the North to the South, they stopped to quench their thirst at the river and unburdened their woes, along with their loads.

"The river birds would fly down to tell Dia stories about ducks who could fly North as far as the Country of the Sands.

"And Dia would remember everything she heard.

"Yet Golo said that Dia was crazy.

"Golo said this to Luke-the-Rabbit. And Luke's loyalty is as shifty as the two slippers he had to put on his head one day so that he could run faster.

"You know, don't you," said Uncle Amadou, "that that's how he got his long ears?

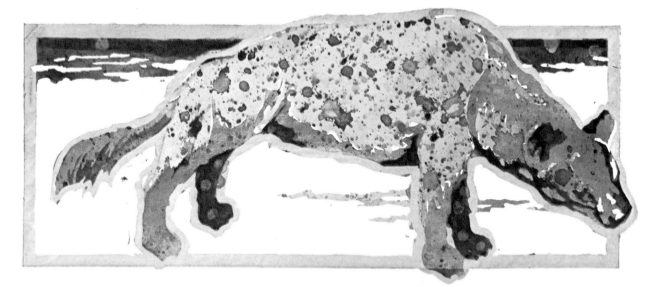

"Golo told Bouki-the-Hyena that Dia was crazy. Bouki acts like a coward or a thief. He slinks around with his backsides bending under him as if he carried a heavy load.

"Golo even told Thio-the-Parrot about Dia. And Thio's round tongue jumps around in her hooked beak tasting all the gossip of the world before she spits it out.

"But the saddest thing is that Golo told Dia's children that Mother Crocodile was crazy. And the little crocodiles believed him.

"When Dia would grow weary from the heat of the sun, she would call her children. When she had grown tired of seeing the moon painting the water half the night she would call her children. And when she saw the little dugouts, their stomachs in the river that runs as fast as the boats, she would call her children.

"She always stopped the little crocodiles from playing to tell them stories. This made the little crocodiles angry.

"But they would listen to Mother Crocodile. The little crocodiles hoped to hear of the great things they would do in the future. They hoped to hear stories of crocodiles. But Mother Crocodile told the little crocodiles stories of times past. She told them stories of men.

"Dia, Mother Crocodile, spoke to her children of hunters and of merchants. She told them of the warriors that their great-grandmama had seen pass and repass on their way to capture slaves and look for gold many, many years ago.

"The little crocodiles listened and yawned. They grew even more angry. And so they chose to believe Golo.

"Dia told them of how men killed the mighty elephants and used their big teeth to make music in their houses or for jewels to adorn their wives.

"She told them how the hunters would kill the handsome zebras and use their skins to cover the floors of men's houses. She told them how Segue-the-Panther fought bravely to keep his family out of men's hands. Men used panther skins for coats.

"And she told them how men hung the heads of animals on walls to decorate them.

"'Why are you telling us these things?' the little crocodiles would ask. 'We are not like those animals. We are tougher.'

"'We must learn from the experiences of others,' Dia would explain. And she kept on telling her tales to her children.

"'Golo said Mama is crazy,' the little crocodiles said. 'He must be right.'

"Still, every day after the sun had traveled to the sea, and the moon had painted half the ocean, Dia called her children to hear her stories.

"She spoke of the coming of men. She spoke of the battles of men with men. She told of how the waters ran red when the men came.

"Once the waters became so red her great-grandmama had to search the muddy bottom of the river for a trail to other waters in which to live.

"And Dia's grandmother had seen wars where hundreds of corpses floated on the water. Then, even the greediest of crocodiles had gotten sick from eating too much. They turned from the sight in disgust. So Dia's grandmother, too, had to search the muddy bottom of the river. She found the trail her mother had followed. It led her to the river where Dia and her children now lived.

"When Dia told these stories, the little crocodiles yawned and yawned. Then they went away to dream.

"They dreamed of faraway rivers where the waters turned up gold nuggets. They dreamed of faraway countries, like Pinkow, where the sun is born. Or they dreamed of countries where crocodiles were gods. Ibis-the-Pilgrim had told them about this, and Ibis was the wisest of all birds.

"They dreamed of the blue river and the white river,

which joined far in the North to become the river they lived in. They dreamed of swimming at the same time in the waters of the two rivers. One side of their bodies lay in the blue river and the other side lay in the white river while the sun caressed their backbones.

"Just like the teeth of their parents, the dreams of the little crocodiles never stopped growing.

"Then one morning a flock of crows passed high over the river. They were crowing:

> A sun completely naked—a sun completely
>   yellow.
> A sun completely naked, sun of early dawn,
> Throws waves of gold on the river,
> The completely yellow river. . . .

"Dia looked up from the bank of the river and saw the crows fly away.

"In the middle of the day other crows came. They flew lower than the first ones. They were crowing:

> A sun completely naked—a sun completely white.
> A sun completely naked, sun of high daylight,
> Throws waves of silver
> On the white river. . . .

"Dia lifted her long jaws and watched the birds fly away. At twilight other crows came. They lit on the bank of the river. They were crowing:

A sun completely naked— a sun completely red.
A sun completely naked and completely red throws
Waves of red blood
On the red river. . . .

"Dia crawled up to them. Her flabby stomach scraped the sand.

"'Why are you flying away?' she asked the crows.

"'War,' the crows told her. 'The men from the West have declared war on the men from the East.'

"Sadly, Dia watched the crows fly away.

"'My children,' she called to the little crocodiles. 'The men from the West have declared war on the men from the East. We must leave at once.'

"'Mama, what is it to us if the men from the West declare war on the men from the East?' her youngest son asked.

"'My child,' Mother Crocodile replied, 'the burning dry weed can inflame the green weed. We must hurry and leave this river.'

"'But we don't want to leave,' the little crocodiles said.

"Dia pleaded. 'My children, I have told you about war, about men killing other men. Where men fight is no place for crocodiles.'

"The little crocodiles closed their eyes and turned their heads. They did not want to listen. Dia cried. But she left by the well-worn trail on the muddy bottom of the river.

"The little crocodiles stayed and played. They swam to the bottom of the river. They swam to the top. They stretched out on the sunny, sandy bank to listen to Golo's chatter.

"'Old talk is crazy talk,' said the mischief-maker Golo. 'You were wise not to listen to crazy Dia.' The little crocodiles nodded their heads.

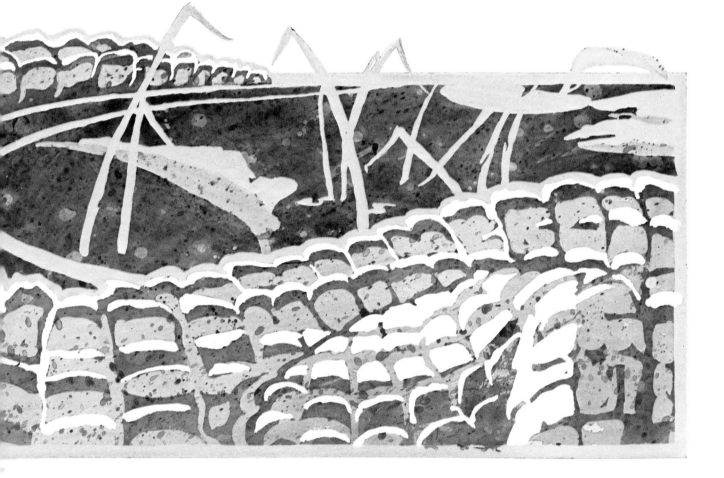

"A shot whizzed by his ear. Golo jumped. The sound of gunfire was everywhere. Golo scampered away. He swung from tree to tree until he found one far away. He sat, his hands over his eyes, on the highest branch.

"Luke-the-Rabbit and all his rabbit children hopped away. Their slippered ears were quivering. They went to hide in a thicket.

"Bouki-the-Hyena and all the little hyenas, their backsides dragging near the ground, headed for distant plains.

"Thio-the-Parrot packed her gossip into her beak. She flew off to a tree in the middle of the forest and hid her head under her wing.

"The men from the West marched up the river. They crossed it in their boats. They landed on the East bank.

"The men from the East pushed them back to the West bank. Back and forth, back and forth the two sides fought.

"The little crocodiles played in the river. With their long mouths they nudged the boats as they crossed the river. They snapped at corpses as they floated downstream. They felt like gods of the waters and thought they had made men their slaves.

"The battle lasted for days. On the seventh day the men from the West stood on the East bank of the river.

"'We have won,' the general of the West rejoiced. 'What gifts of conquest shall we take home to our wives?'

"His aide replied: 'What better gifts than purses? Purses made from the skins of crocodiles!' The men from the West picked up their rifles.

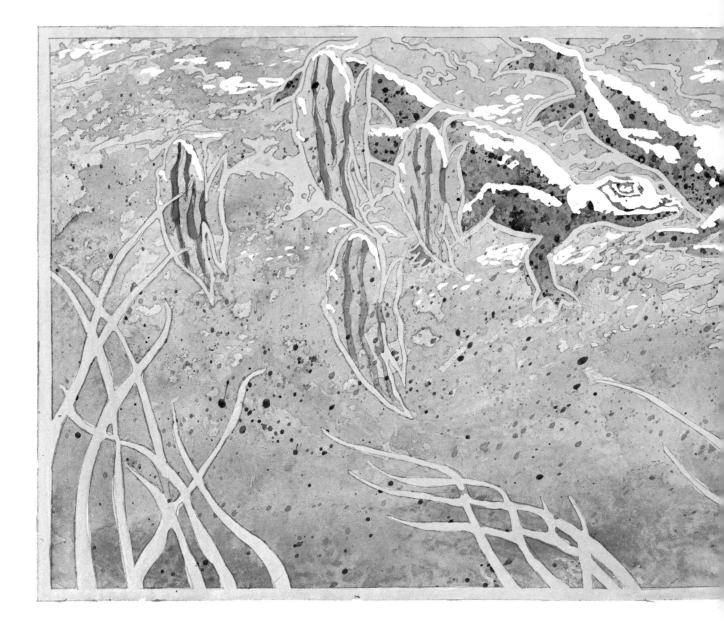

"Bullets fell to the right of the little crocodiles. They swam to the left. Bullets fell to the left. The little crocodiles swam to the muddy bottom of the river. The soldiers spread a net over the water. The men knew that little crocodiles must rise for air.

"The two younger crocodiles began to cry. But the oldest thought of his mama. He remembered Dia's tales of their grandmama. He remembered Dia's tales of their great-grandmama. 'Follow me,' he cried. They searched, and before their breath gave out, found the well-worn trail.

"It is true," said Uncle Amadou, rising and knocking his pipe clean, "that old talk can sometimes sound crazy. But it is my opinion that when little crocodiles close their ears, their skins may someday cost them dear."

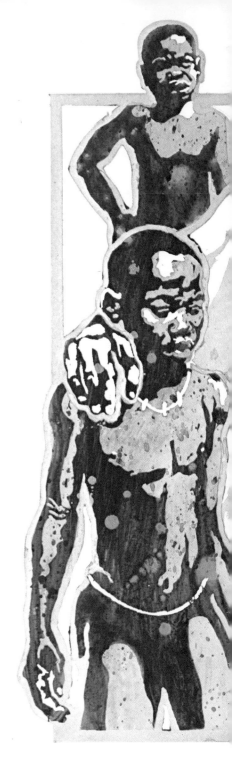

Born in Dakar, Senegal, in 1906, **Birago Diop** studied in France. After his return to Africa, he worked as a veterinarian, wrote poetry, and was ambassador to Tunisia. Amadou Koumba was the household storyteller (or *griot*) in Mr. Diop's grandmother's house. Mr. Diop says, "Amadou Koumba recounted to me the tales that had lulled me to sleep as a child. He taught me others, too, studded with maxims and morals, in which can be found all the wisdom of our ancestors." Mr. Diop has rendered many of these tales into French.

Rosa Guy, who had heard of his work, met Mr. Diop on a recent trip to Senegal. She decided to translate and adapt "Maman-Caïman" into English from the French to give English-speaking children a glimpse of the richness of African folklore and history. *Mother Crocodile* is Ms. Guy's first picture book.

The illustrator of *Mother Crocodile,* **John Steptoe,** is well known for the many innovative books he has written and illustrated. The boldly conceived paintings here are a departure from his usual contemporary style. Working in watercolor and influenced by Japanese art, he sought to derive the simplest of forms from the complexity of nature.

ABOUT THE BOOK

The text type used in *Mother Crocodile* is Goudy Old Style. The title on the jacket, half-title, and title page was hand-lettered by David Gatti. The four-color art was camera-separated by Mueller Color Plate Company. The book was printed by A. Hoen & Co. and bound by Economy Bookbinding Corporation.